I Am a Yogi—

My First Book of Yoga

Written and illustrated by
ANNE COX

I AM A YOGI - MY FIRST BOOK OF YOGA

Summary: A sequence of yoga poses teaches
children to move and breathe with intention.
(1. Yoga-non-fiction   2.Children-non-fiction)

Archway Publishing books may be ordered through booksellers or by contacting:

Archway Publishing
1663 Liberty Drive
Bloomington, IN 47403
www.archwaypublishing.com
1-(888)-242-5904

Because of the dynamic nature of the Internet, any web addresses or links contained
in this book may have changed since publication and may no longer be valid. The views
expressed in this work are solely those of the author and do not necessarily reflect the
views of the publisher, and the publisher hereby disclaims any responsibility for them.

ISBN: 978-1-4808-0760-0 (sc)
ISBN: 978-1-4808-0761-7 (hc)
ISBN: 978-1-4808-0759-4 (e)

Library of Congress Control Number: 2014908897

Printed in the United States of America

Archway Publishing rev. date: 05/19/2014

Yoga means yoke or join.

A yoga mat is a private space for a child to practice self discipline. It gives him/her freedom and control over 'self', within limits.

Yoga sequencing flows together and helps improve memory and extend one's attention span.

Remembering to breathe establishes rhythm and provides strength with movement.

For
KILIAN, WAYLON and CECILIA

FOREWORD

Anne Cox's I AM A YOGI—MY FIRST BOOK OF YOGA is dynamically written in first person, from the child's point of view.

Her delightful vintage paper doll illustrations invite the child to play along, STRETCHING, BREATHING, ROCKING, BREATHING, RESTING, BREATHING.

From ROLLING out the mat, to NAMASTE, the child practices one FLOWING sequence that is easy to READ and to memorize.

Moving with intention and purpose is EFFECTIVE for lengthening attention span and self-soothing.

I AM A YOGI—MY FIRST BOOK OF YOGA will plant a seed in a child's imagination that will continue flowering and bearing fruit for a lifetime.

—Julie Carmen, MA, LMFT, ERYT-500

Julie Carmen starred in dozens of Hollywood films and danced on Broadway off Broadway. She holds a Masters in Clinical Psychology, is a licensed Marriage and Family Therapist, certified Yoga Therapist, ERYT-500 and founded Yoga Talks, a yoga media production company. www.yogatalks.com

This is my yoga mat.

I roll it out on the floor.

I sit on my mat with
my legs crossed.

This is called
SUKASANA or EASY POSE.

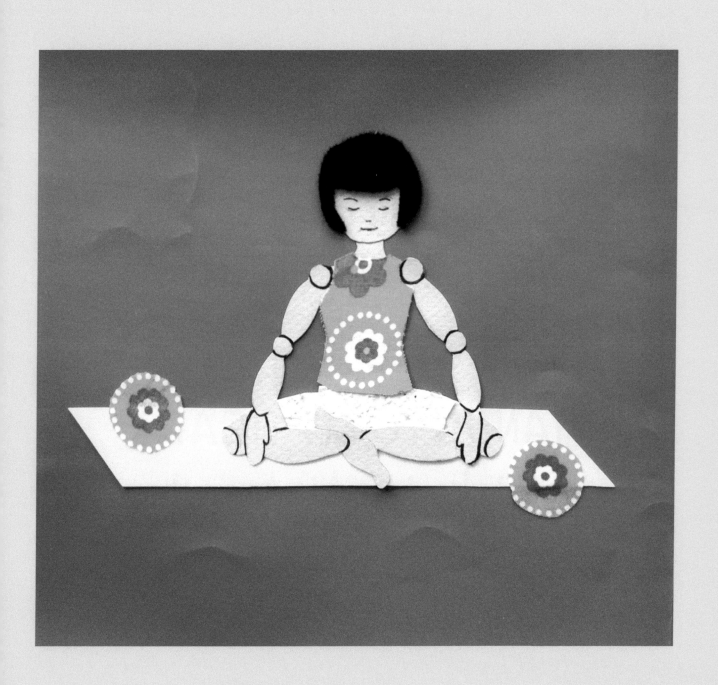

I reach my arms up to
GATHER MY ENERGY.

I bring my
HANDS TO MY HEART
and take two big breaths.

I come to my knees and hands for
TABLE POSE.

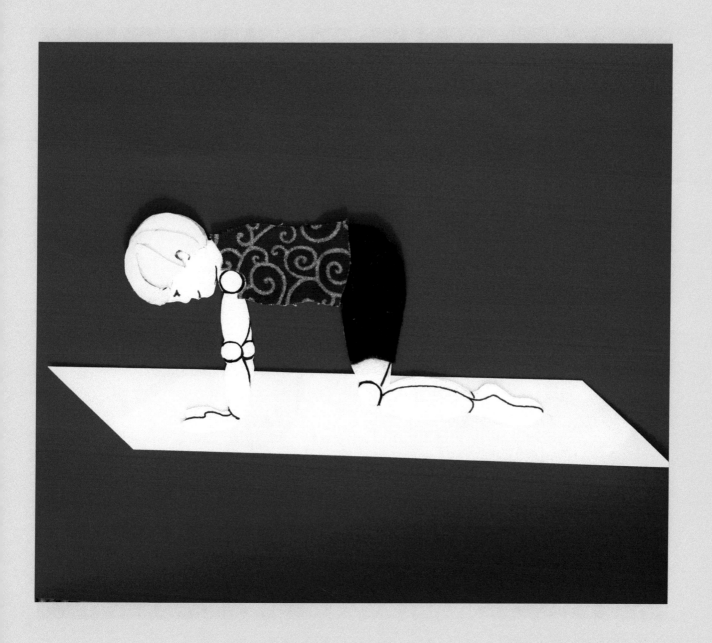

I puff out my tummy and take a BIG BREATH through my nose.

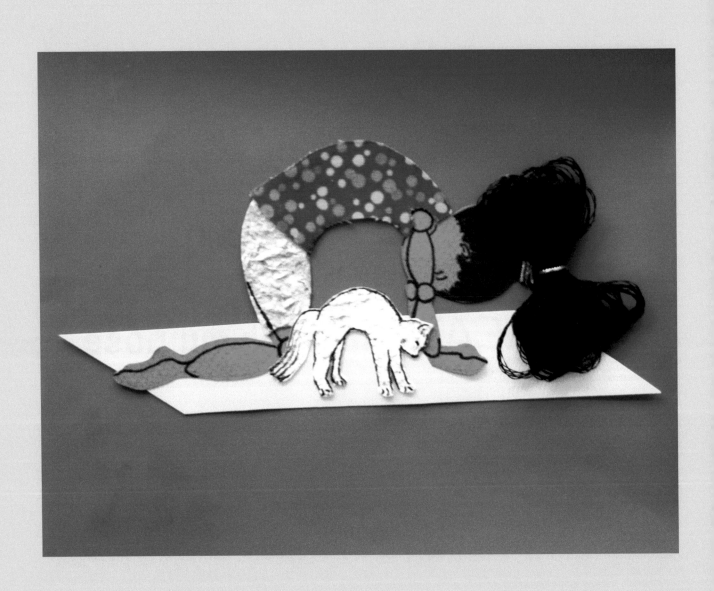

Then I arch my back like a scary CAT and blow out all the air.

With my hands on the mat,
I push up to my tiptoes and
stretch my bottom to the sky.

This is DOWNWARD
FACING DOG pose.

I lift my leg up to the sky,
wag it like a DOG'S TAIL and
bring it back to the floor.

Then I do the other leg.

Now, I lie down on my tummy and fold my arms under my head.

My feet turn out and I rest, breathing in and out like a big green CROCODILE.

I roll to my back. I bend my knees and hold my feet with my hands and rock side to side.

I am in HAPPY BABY pose.

I roll to my side and
up on my knees.

My head is on the mat
in BALASANA or the
POSE OF A CHILD.

I take two more big breaths.

I reach my arms up to the sky. I gather my energy and put my hands together.

I bring them to my heart and say, "NAMASTE."

Namaste is used as a sign of seeing goodness in `self´ and in others.

It means "bow me you" in sanskrit, an ancient language of India.

a	arch	lie	
air	arms	lift	
all	back	move	
am	bend	'namaste'	
and	bottom	nose	
baby	blow	now	
book	breath (s)	other	
big	breathe (ing)	pose	
can	called	puff	
cat	child	push	
do	come	reach	Sanskrit
dog	crocodile	rest	
for	crossed	rock	
I	down (ward)	roll (ing)	Balasana
in	easy	scary	Sukasana
is	energy	side	Namaste
it	facing	sky	
like	feet	stretch	
mat	first	table	
of	floor	tail	
on	fold	take	
or	gather	then	
out	green	through	
sit	hands	tiptoes	
the	happy	tummy	
this	head	turn	
to	heart	under	
two	hold	wag	
up	knees	yoga	
with	legs	yogi	

ACKNOWLEDGMENTS

For their inspiration, I thank my grandchildren: Kilian, Waylon, Cecilia, Clayton, Grant, Addison, Isabelle, Kai, Paloma, Desirae, Danielle and Ethan; my husband Bill Compere, Jenny Laper and Julie Carmen for encouraging me to "get this published" and my father, Charles Singleton, for underwriting it.

For their advice and expertise in their respective fields, I thank Michal Dale BS/Ed & MA/media, Cyndi Freeman MS/Ed, and my Guru and inspiring yoga teacher, Beth Spindler ERYT/500, for her deep knowledge and methods of helping me "get" what yoga really is.

For believing in me and for their kind words, I thank Julie Carmen, "choreographer of living" and David Harrison, renowned children's author.

"Together, we can make it happen" to my publishing team, Adriane, Casey and Madison.

Deepest gratitude, Anne

ABOUT THE AUTHOR

Photo by Josh Mitchell

Anne Cox is an artist, writer and yoga teacher who has lived in Japan, Kansas, Pennsylvania and Missouri. She has traveled the world and now lives in Springfield, Missouri with her husband, Bill. She has a Bachelor's of Fine Arts degree, a diploma from the Institute of Children's Literature and a 500 Hour Certification from the Registered Yoga Alliance.